THE HUMAN PATH
ACROSS THE CONTINENTS

PATHWAYS THROUGH
ANTARCTICA

John C. Miles

CRABTREE
PUBLISHING COMPANY
WWW.CRABTREEBOOKS.COM

CRABTREE
PUBLISHING COMPANY
WWW.CRABTREEBOOKS.COM

Author: John C. Miles

Editorial director: Kathy Middleton

Editors: Rachel Cooke, Janine Deschenes

Design: Jeni Child

Photo research:
 FFP Consulting; Tammy McGarr

Proofreader: Melissa Boyce

Print and production coordinator:
 Katherine Berti

Produced for Crabtree Publishing Company by
FFP Consulting Limited

Images
t=Top, b=Bottom, tl=Top Left, tr=Top Right,
bl=Bottom Left, br=Bottom Right, c=Center,
lc=Left Center, rc=Right Center

Alamy
 Classic Image: p. 10bl; Lordprice Collection:
 p. 11t; Cavan Images: p. 11rc; INTERFOTO:
 p. 12t; Eye Ubiquitous p. 17t; NG Images:
 p. 22t; ZUMA Press, Inc.: p. 26b; Cavan
 Images: p. 27b; ARCTIC IMAGES: p. 29rc
AP Images
 An xin - Imaginechina: p. 27t
British Antarctic Survey
 Adam Bradley: p. 21rc;
 Robert Mulvaney: p. 23br
Getty
 Imagno / Contributor: p. 14
iStock
 ZU_09: p. 8b; duncan1890: p. 9lc;
 Elenarts: p. 10br

NASA
 NASA Earth Observatory image by Jesse
 Allen, using Landsat data from the U.S.
 Geological Survey: p. 7t
**National Institute of Water and Atmospheric
 Research, New Zealand**
 Dave Allen: p. 18
Shutterstock
 I. Noyan Yilmaz: p. 5b; Sergey Goryachev
 p. 13b; CherylRamalho: p. 21b;
 MarcAndreLeTourneux p. 25t
Wikimedia Commons
 National Maritime Museum p. 6; PD-ART:
 p. 7b; Paramount: p. 15tr; National Museum
 of the US Navy: p. 15bl

All other images from Shutterstock

Maps: Jeni Child

Library and Archives Canada Cataloguing in Publication

Title: Pathways through Antarctica / John C. Miles.
Names: Miles, John C., 1960- author.
Description: Series statement: The human path across the continents |
 Includes index.
Identifiers: Canadiana (print) 20190112026 | Canadiana (ebook) 20190112034
 ISBN 9780778766001 (hardcover)
 ISBN 9780778766452 (softcover)
 ISBN 9781427123978 (HTML)
Subjects: LCSH: Human ecology—Antarctica—Juvenile literature. |
 LCSH: Antarctica—Juvenile literature.
Classification: LCC GF891 .M55 2019 | DDC j304.209989—dc23

Library of Congress Cataloging-in-Publication Data

CIP available at the Library of Congress

LCCN 2019023322

Crabtree Publishing Company

Printed in the U.S.A./082019/CG20190712

www.crabtreebooks.com   1-800-387-7650

Published in Canada
Crabtree Publishing
616 Welland Ave.
St. Catharines, Ontario
L2M 5V6

Published in the United States
Crabtree Publishing
PMB 59051
350 Fifth Avenue, 59th Floor
New York, New York 10118

Published in the United Kingdom
Crabtree Publishing
Maritime House
Basin Road North, Hove
BN41 1WR

Published in Australia
Crabtree Publishing
Unit 3–5 Currumbin Court
Capalaba
QLD 4157

CONTENTS

ANTARCTICA

The Human Path Across
ANTARCTICA

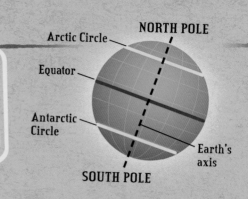

NORTH POLE
Arctic Circle
Equator
Antarctic Circle
Earth's axis
SOUTH POLE

Welcome to the coldest place on Earth—Antarctica. With an area about 1.5 times the size of the United States, Antarctica is the world's fifth-largest continent. The extremely cold climate makes it difficult for people to survive there. Only since the mid-1900s has technology allowed humans to stay in Antarctica long enough to explore its geography and study its wildlife.

Glacier in Antarctica

THE AVERAGE TEMPERATURE in Antarctica is always low enough to freeze water. When snow falls in Antarctica, it doesn't melt, but builds up year after year. Over the centuries, this has created a covering of ice. In winter, temperatures can fall as low as –80°F (–62°C). No animals live in the middle of Antarctica. But on the edge of the continent and in the seas that surround it, whales, fish, seabirds, and penguins have all adapted to the extreme environment.

Antarctica has just two seasons—summer and winter. Summer runs from November to February; winter from March to October. In summer, the Sun never sets. There is no darkness. In winter, there is no daylight. The Sun never rises.

ANTARCTICA sits below the **Antarctic Circle**—Earth's southernmost circle of **latitude**. The continent is surrounded by some of the planet's stormiest seas. 98 percent of the land is covered by ice. Floating **ice shelves** surround about 11 percent of Antarctica's 11,100-mile (17,900 km) coastline. Thick sea ice extends into the surrounding ocean.

Underneath Antarctica is a base of ancient rock. In some places, mountain ranges soar to more than 15,000 feet (4,500 m) high. Antarctica contains the **geographic South Pole,** which is found on the flat, barren **Antarctic Plateau** at 90 degrees south.

Humpback whale in Antarctica

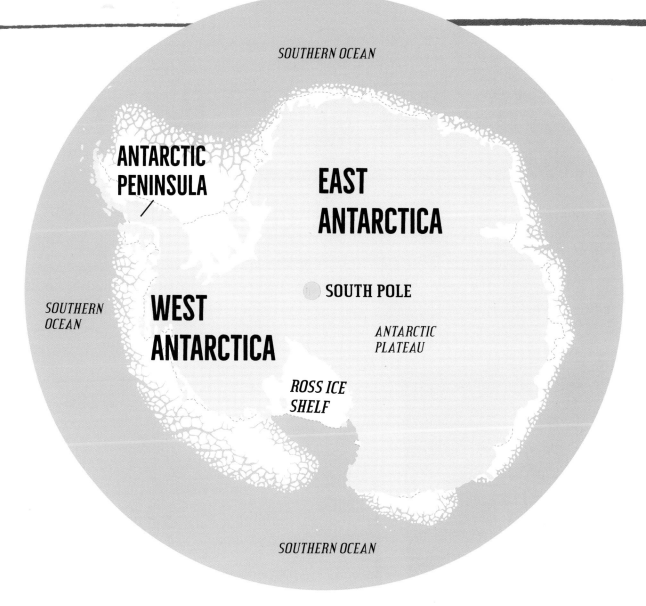

SOUTHERN OCEAN

ANTARCTIC
PENINSULA

EAST
ANTARCTICA

SOUTHERN
OCEAN

WEST
ANTARCTICA

SOUTH POLE

ANTARCTIC
PLATEAU

ROSS ICE
SHELF

SOUTHERN OCEAN

SCIENTISTS from many countries travel to Antarctica to live and work at research stations. There, they carry out work to learn more about Antarctica's environment and the impact of **climate change**. Some of these settlements are permanent but, even so, only about 1,000 people live in Antarctica all year round.

This book explores Antarctica through a series of human journeys. Some of these are historical. They demonstrate how people slowly learned about Antarctica and its riches—and dangers—through exploration. Other journeys are modern, and reveal the kinds of trips that people make in Antarctica today.

Scientists at work, Weddell Sea, Antarctica

POLARSTERN

Sail to
THE EDGE OF THE ICE

Hundreds of years ago, vast areas of Earth were unknown to many people. The Antarctic region was unexplored. There were rumors of a continent at the southern tip of the world. During the 1500s, some European explorers began traveling south to find out if these rumors were true. In the eighteenth century, British explorer Captain James Cook was the first to sail ships into the seas around Antarctica.

Captain James Cook, painting from 1776

Cook's second voyage

AFRICA

ATLANTIC OCEAN

INDIAN OCEAN

SOUTH AMERICA

ANTARCTICA

PACIFIC OCEAN

NEW ZEALAND

AUSTRALIA

↑ **CAPTAIN JAMES COOK (1728-1779)** sailed around the world in three famous voyages. He made maps of islands, coastlines, and other geographical features. Cook set off from England in July 1772 on his second trip with two ships, HMS *Resolution* and HMS *Adventure*. He aimed to sail as far south as possible to discover if the claims about a southern continent were true.

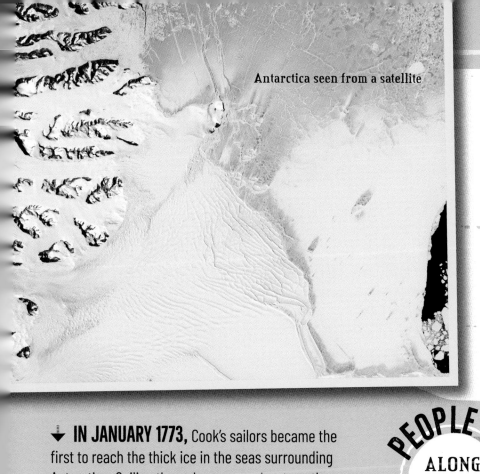

Antarctica seen from a satellite

◀ **MAKING ACCURATE MAPS**
in the 1700s was difficult and time-consuming. First, sailors made on-the-spot observations. They then used **surveying** tools to calculate the size of geographical features, such as hills. The process could take months. Today's mapmakers use **satellite** imaging and data to map Earth's surface in great detail. An area that once would have taken many months to survey can today be mapped in hours or even minutes.

▼ **IN JANUARY 1773,** Cook's sailors became the first to reach the thick ice in the seas surrounding Antarctica. Sailing through unmapped waters, they observed seabirds, penguins, and whales. Cook returned the next year to try and find a way through the ice, but this wasn't possible. On a later voyage, he mapped many of the islands surrounding Antarctica. Although James Cook never actually saw the continent on his voyages, one thing became clear—finding out more about what lay at the southern tip of the globe was not going to be easy.

PEOPLE ALONG THE WAY

Cook was amazed by the extent of the ice shelves he saw on his voyage. They stretched far beyond his sight and were dazzling in the sunlight. He was sure that the ice shelves reached as far as the South Pole, and guessed that they were indeed joined to a southern continent.

1777 engraving of Cook's ship near an iceberg

Discovering A NEW CONTINENT

Throughout the nineteenth century, people traveled to Antarctica on voyages that often took them away from home for years. Some wanted to benefit from the region's **natural resources.** Others were scientists who wanted to find out more about Antarctica.

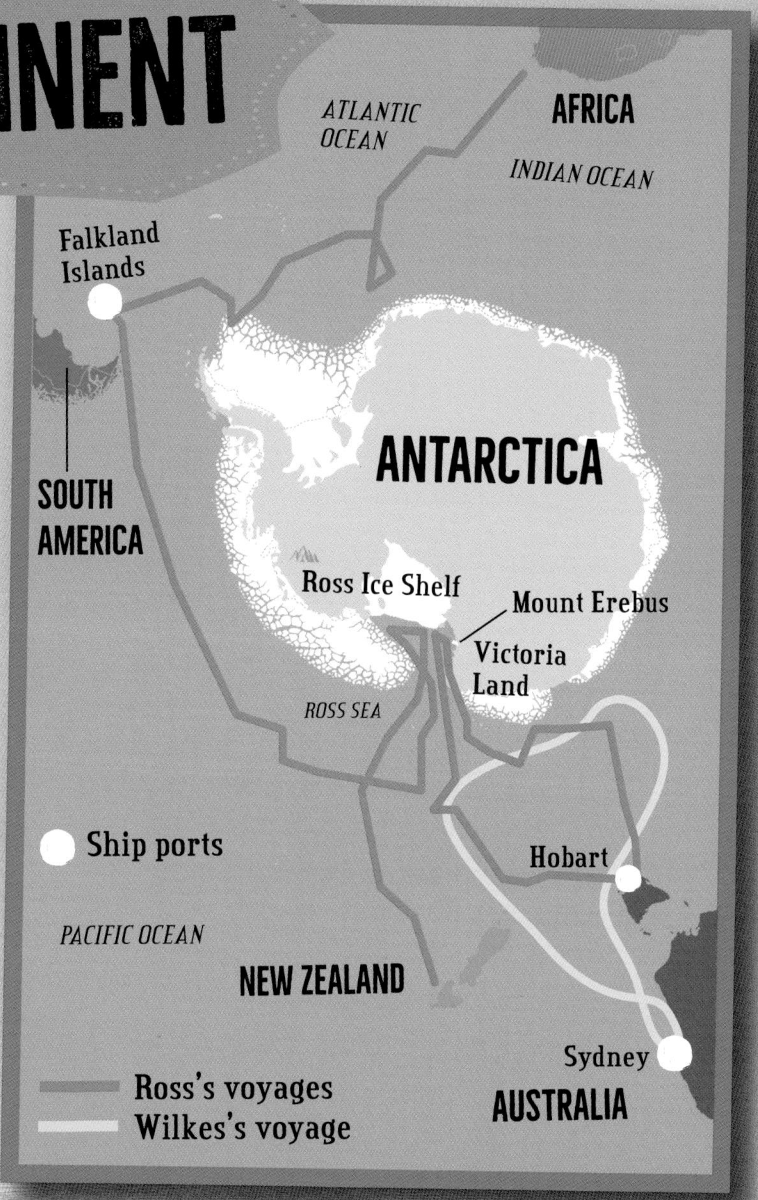
ATLANTIC OCEAN
AFRICA
INDIAN OCEAN
Falkland Islands
ANTARCTICA
SOUTH AMERICA
Ross Ice Shelf
Mount Erebus
Victoria Land
ROSS SEA
Ship ports
Hobart
PACIFIC OCEAN
NEW ZEALAND
Sydney
Ross's voyages
Wilkes's voyage
AUSTRALIA

WHALES AND SEALS in the Antarctic region were hunted ruthlessly in the early 1800s. Whale fat was made into oil that was burned in lamps. Seal fur was used to make coats and mittens. From the late 1700s, many European whale and seal hunters lived in camps on remote islands in the seas surrounding Antarctica. By 1822, the southern fur seal had been so heavily hunted that it was **extinct** in many areas.

Whale hunters in action, illustration from 1869

THE UNITED STATES expedition of 1838, led by **naval officer** Charles Wilkes, reached Antarctica in 1840. The expedition investigated a huge area of coastline covered with **glaciers**. These massive structures are made up of thick, dense ice, loose rock, and water. Glaciers are constantly on the move. They slowly slide down slopes and valleys under their own weight. Wilkes was the first explorer to prove that Antarctica was a continent.

Glacier in Antarctica

Pulling a ship through the ice, nineteenth-century illustration

SIR JAMES CLARK ROSS (1800–1862) was a British explorer. In 1839, he set off from England to lead a scientific expedition to Antarctica. In 1841, he discovered the Ross Sea and Victoria Land, a mountainous region in Antarctica. His discovery proved beyond all doubt that Antarctica was a rocky continent covered by ice.

Ross's explorations also revealed mountain ranges and even active volcanoes. Mount Erebus, named after one of his ships, the HMS *Erebus*, is the southernmost volcano in the world. Ross's ships sailed for 250 miles (400 km) along a coastline of solid ice, which he named "The Great Ice Barrier." Today, this area is known as the Ross Ice Shelf.

PEOPLE

ALONG THE WAY

Ross's ships were **reinforced** so they could withstand hitting ice. Ross was glad, as he took his ships deep into the packed ice around Antarctica. He described the ice as frightening. He knew his ships could not sail through the vast area of the Ross Ice Shelf, which he said was like cliffs of stone.

Mount Erebus

Ski to the
SOUTH POLE

ANTARCTICA

ROSS SEA

Bay of
Whales

*ROSS ICE
SHELF*

SOUTH POLE

—— Amundsen's route

By the early 1900s, one of the major aims of Antarctic exploration was to reach the South Pole. It took until 1911 for explorers to overcome the huge challenges of this journey.

↓ NORWEGIAN EXPLORER ROALD AMUNDSEN (1872-1928)

first traveled to Antarctica with the Belgian Antarctic Expedition of 1897 to 1899. The expedition had to spend the winter in Antarctica when their ship, the *Belgica*, got locked in ice. American doctor Frederick Cook kept crew members healthy by hunting animals for fresh meat. This saved the crew from the deadly disease **scurvy**.

Roald Amundsen

After surviving a winter in Antarctica, Amundsen also spent two winters in Nunavut in northern Canada. There he learned survival skills from the **Inuit**. He learned how to drive dog **sleds**, and discovered that animal-skin clothing was the best way to stay warm. The lessons he learned from the Inuit were important.

Dogs pulling sleds

Amundsen's team at the South Pole, 1911

Mountain bike rider in Antarctica

▲ AMUNDSEN'S SOUTH POLE EXPEDITION

arrived at the Ross Ice Shelf in January 1911, and set up a **base camp** in the Bay of Whales. They prepared supplies and equipment and built **supply depots** along the route to the South Pole. Then, on October 19, 1911, they set off with four sleds and 52 dogs. Amundsen planned to kill many of the dogs to supply his men with fresh meat.

Moving ahead on sleds and skis, the team arrived at the South Pole on December 14. After setting up a small tent and leaving a letter for anyone who might arrive at the pole in the future, Amundsen and his men began the return journey. They arrived back at base camp on January 25, 1912, with 11 surviving dogs. The South Pole had finally been conquered.

PEOPLE
ALONG THE WAY

Amundsen planned carefully for his journey and felt his success was largely due to his excellent equipment. For example, he carefully chose the best ski boots and skis for the expedition. He and his men ate foods that would give them enough strength for the difficult journey to the South Pole.

▲ MODERN COMMUNICATION EQUIPMENT

and warm clothing have helped many adventurers make amazing journeys to the South Pole in recent times. In 1993, Norwegian Erling Kagge made a solo trip on skis. The following year, Liv Arnesen became the first woman to do the same. Two more unusual journeys took place in 2014. The Netherlands' Manon Ossevoort drove the 2,882-mile (4,638 km) round trip in a farm tractor, and American Daniel Burton rode a bicycle to the South Pole.

Battle Against ANTARCTIC STORMS

In **1910**, British explorer Robert Falcon Scott (**1868-1912**) set out to reach the South Pole. At first, Scott was unaware that Amundsen was planning to do the same thing. But a combination of planning failures and bad luck meant that Scott's Antarctic expedition ended in tragedy.

Scott's men hauling sleds, 1911

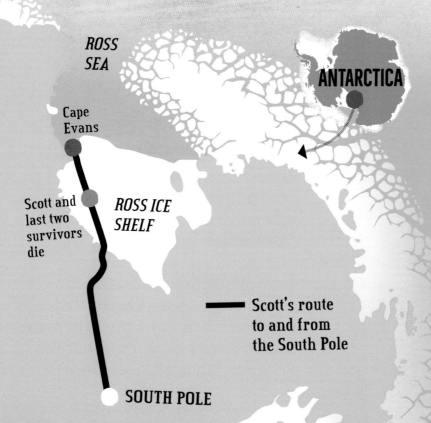

ROSS SEA

ANTARCTICA

Cape Evans

Scott and last two survivors die

ROSS ICE SHELF

— Scott's route to and from the South Pole

SOUTH POLE

▲ **SCOTT'S EXPEDITION** used a variety of transportation methods. He used ponies and dogs to haul sleds to the South Pole. But the ponies were unhealthy and unfamiliar with the cold. Many had to be shot. Scott also experimented with early motorized sleds, which broke down.

After a huge storm, Scott's ship, the *Terra Nova*, was frozen in the Antarctic ice for 20 days. This left less time to prepare for the South Pole journey before winter set in. Scott's men established a base camp at Cape Evans in January 1911, and began to set up supply depots on the route to the South Pole.

Geographic South Pole

Roald Amundsen		Robert F. Scott
December 14 1911		January 17, 1912
"So we arrived and were able to plant our flag at the geographical South Pole."		"The Pole. Yes, but under very different circumstances from those expected."

elevation 9,301 feet

SCOTT'S BASE CAMP HUT still stands today as a memorial to the expedition. Scott and his team were seen as heroes, but their tragic end showed how important it was to have adequate supplies and suitable transportation to travel across Antarctica. Reliable aircraft would prove a huge help, but in 1912, these were many years in the future.

⬆ **IN NOVEMBER 1911,** Scott and his men set off in small groups. They took turns pulling the heavy sleds. After an exhausting journey in terrible weather, a five-man team, led by Scott, reached the South Pole on January 17, 1912. There they found Amundsen's tent and letter, which was left behind just five weeks earlier.

On the 800-mile (1,300 km) return journey, the weather worsened. By February 7, Scott and his men had covered 300 miles (480 km), but food and fuel were running out. Everyone was suffering from terrible **frostbite**. Scott's party began to weaken and die. The last three survivors, including Scott, stopped 150 miles (240 km) short of their base camp and just 11 miles (18 km) from a supply depot. They froze to death in their tent.

Scott's base camp hut

Pause for
REFLECTION

- Why do you think Scott's expedition ended the way it did? What could he have done to avoid the tragedy?
- How did Amundsen's expedition planning differ from Scott's?
- Imagine you are planning an expedition to the South Pole today. What would you take with you?

Postage stamp showing Scott (center top) at the South Pole

1ST

SCOTT EXPEDITION
1912 SOUTH POLE

A Flight Over ANTARCTICA

ROSS SEA

ROSS ICE SHELF

Bay of Whales

FORD RANGES

ROSS ICE SHELF

Little America

ROCKEFELLER PLATEAU

— Plane journey

SOUTH POLE

In 1929, American naval officer Richard E. Byrd became the first person to fly an aircraft to the South Pole and back. This was the beginning of a new era for Antarctic exploration. New technologies helped humans overcome the challenges of Antarctica.

⬇ **RICHARD EVELYN BYRD (1888-1957)** joined the U.S. Navy and served in World War I. After the war, he became interested in polar exploration. He claimed to have flown over the North Pole in 1926. Byrd's first Antarctic expedition of 1928 to 1930 was large and well-funded. Backers including Ford Motor Company president Edsel Ford and banker John D. Rockefeller helped pay for the expedition. From their Little America base camp on the Ross Ice Shelf, the expedition recorded weather, took photographs, and investigated Antarctic rocks.

Byrd in his plane using a sextant to navigate across Antarctica

BYRD'S AIRPLANE was named the *Floyd Bennett*. On November 28, 1929, Byrd and three crew members flew it from their base to the South Pole and back. The plane was weighed down with extra fuel and supplies, and had trouble lifting high enough to fly over the Antarctic Plateau. The men were forced to dump some cargo to lighten it. The flight returned safely after 18 hours and 41 minutes.

Byrd's Antarctic flights revealed many new features, such as the Rockefeller Mountains, the Rockefeller Plateau, and the Ford mountain ranges—all named after the expedition's financial supporters.

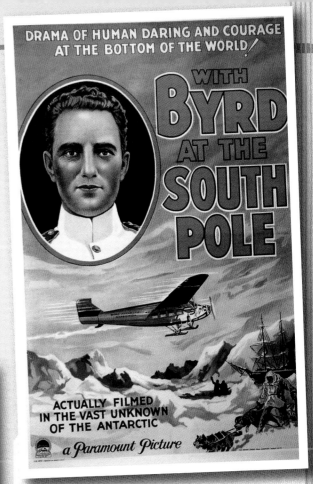

DRAMA OF HUMAN DARING AND COURAGE AT THE BOTTOM OF THE WORLD!

WITH **BYRD** AT THE **SOUTH POLE**

ACTUALLY FILMED IN THE VAST UNKNOWN OF THE ANTARCTIC

a Paramount Picture

Movie poster from 1930

Byrd with the *Floyd Bennett*

BYRD LED further expeditions to the Antarctic in 1933 and 1939. In 1946, he led the largest Antarctic expedition to date, with 4,000 people, 15 ships, and many aircraft. He explored the eastern part of the continent, and discovered 10 new mountain ranges. Byrd used radio broadcasting to help make people aware of his work. He even starred in a movie documentary—*With Byrd at the South Pole*—which won an Academy Award in 1930.

Many technologies developed rapidly in the twentieth century to help scientists explore Antarctica. These included aircraft, radio, and **aerial photography**. Today, aircraft transport supplies and scientists to and from research stations and areas of exploration.

Pause for REFLECTION

- How has the use of aircraft helped those who live and work in Antarctica?
- Why do you think it is important for scientists to tell people about their research in Antarctica?

15

Fly to the SOUTH POLE Today

South Pole Traverse

ANTARCTIC PENINSULA

EAST ANTARCTICA

WEST ANTARCTICA

SOUTH POLE
Amundsen-Scott
South Pole Station

ROSS ICE SHELF

McMurdo Station

ROSS SEA

Since the 1950s, better technology has made it easier for humans to explore and work in Antarctica. For example, modern aircraft and cold-resistant clothing have made it safer to travel there. Today, more than 40 nations have set up research stations on the continent.

Amundsen-Scott South Pole Station is operated by the United States all year round. In summer, about 150 people live and work there. In winter, this drops to around 45 people. Because of harsh winter weather, the station is almost impossible to get to.

⬇ **TO REACH** Amundsen-Scott South Pole Station, people travel from New Zealand to the McMurdo Station, located on the edge of the Ross Sea. McMurdo Station has three runways and includes the world's southernmost harbor. Aircraft making the journey from McMurdo have special skis that allow them to land on snow and ice. The flight to Amundsen-Scott takes about three hours each way.

Hercules aircraft landing at the South Pole

Amundsen-Scott South Pole Station

▶ **THE SCIENTISTS** who work at Amundsen-Scott South Pole Station research areas such as weather and climate, glaciology (the study of glaciers), space science, and **astronomy**. Support staff—such as cooks and engineers—also work there.

The South Pole is an excellent place for looking into space. The South Pole Telescope is a massive telescope situated at Amundsen-Scott South Pole Station. Scientists use the telescope's cameras to make maps of huge areas of sky and to search for stars and galaxies.

Tractor on the South Pole Traverse

◀ **THE SOUTH POLE TRAVERSE** is a highway between McMurdo Station and Amundsen-Scott South Pole Station. It was built by the United States National Science Foundation in the early 2000s to reduce the pollution from flights to the South Pole. This 995-mile (1600 km) road is made of compacted ice. It allows special tractors to deliver supplies and equipment to the South Pole. The trip takes about 40 days.

PEOPLE ALONG THE WAY

Tom is a researcher at Amundsen-Scott South Pole Station. To survive outdoors at the South Pole, he needs to wear layers. First, he puts on two layers of clothing to trap his body heat. Then, he adds a hooded outer layer such as a **parka**. It keeps out wind and water. Warm gloves, boots, and a hat with ear coverings help keep cold out. Finally, he wears goggles to protect his eyes from the glare of the Sun on the ice.

Boat Across the SOUTHERN OCEAN

New Zealand is one of many countries that carry out climate and ocean research in Antarctica. Scientists from New Zealand regularly travel to Antarctica and the seas around it on fact-finding voyages.

AUSTRALIA

Southern Ocean

NEW ZEALAND

Wellington

ANTARCTICA

RV *Tangaroa* at sea

◄ **RV TANGAROA** is New Zealand's deepwater research ship. The *Tangaroa* is a good example of the type of ship needed for scientific work in Antarctica. The ship is 230 feet (70 m) long. It has a specially strengthened **hull** and powerful engines to allow it to push through sea ice. It has **sonar** equipment that allows scientists to see what lies on the ocean floor. The ship also carries special equipment that takes **samples** of marine life.

A camp on the ice set up by scientists to study global warming

↑ NEW ZEALAND SCIENTISTS traveling to Antarctica take water samples from the Southern Ocean, make weather observations, monitor pollution, and study ocean animals, such as whales. Some scientists investigate the Southern Ocean's **plankton**. These tiny plants and animals drift around in the ocean, and are then eaten by larger creatures. A healthy plankton population can show that the rest of an ocean's ecosystem is healthy too.

Average temperatures on Earth are rising. This is called **global warming**. Scientists in Antarctica study this change. A big effect of global warming in Antarctica is melting ice. Species such as the Emperor penguin depend on the ice for survival. Studying the effects of global warming in Antarctica helps scientists predict how the issue will affect Earth in the future.

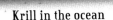

Krill in the ocean

↑ KRILL are small, shrimp-like creatures that exist in vast numbers in Antarctic seas. They are food for whales, seals, penguins, squid, and many kinds of fish. They are a key part of Antarctic **food chains**. Scientists studying the Southern Ocean have discovered that krill numbers are in decline. This is partly because krill feed on algae that grow on the underside of Antarctic ice. With less ice in and around Antarctica due to global warming, there is less food for the krill to eat.

PEOPLE

ALONG THE WAY

Manju is a **marine biologist** from New Zealand. Her work is to study whale populations in the Southern Ocean. Manju has made the Antarctic journey twice. Her best memories of the voyages are the size and colors of the towering icebergs the ship passes, and the sound of the *Tangaroa* crunching through sea ice.

A Trip TO BIRD ISLAND

The rocky islands in the seas surrounding Antarctica lie far from any human settlement. In the 1800s, many of these lonely places were bases for whale and seal hunting. Today, scientists travel to the islands to study the wide range of birds and mammals that live there.

↑ **SOUTH GEORGIA ISLAND** is part of a remote group of islands in the South Atlantic Ocean. It is a British territory. South Georgia is rocky and cold, with mountains covered by snow. The seas around South Georgia have been a Marine Protected Area since 2012. This means there are strict limits in place on **commercial** fishing, in order to help fish species survive.

FALKLAND ISLANDS

SOUTH AMERICA

SOUTH GEORGIA ISLAND

ANTARCTIC PENINSULA

BIRD ISLAND

SOUTH GEORGIA

A pair of wandering albatrosses

Pause for
REFLECTION

- Why do scientists think it is important to protect areas of wilderness?
- What are some steps taken to preserve the environment on and near Bird Island?
- What can people do to reduce plastic pollution in oceans and rivers?

⬆ **BIRD ISLAND** was first discovered by James Cook in 1775. It is a short distance from South Georgia and home to thousands of seabirds and seals. The island is just 3 miles (4.8 km) long. Today, it is a Site of Special Scientific Interest (a type of protected area) due to the amount of rare birdlife there. Since the 1980s, Bird Island has been home to a year-round research station of the British Antarctic Survey, a scientific research organization.

Bird Island and South Georgia can only be reached by sea. Travel to the islands is strictly controlled so wildlife is disturbed as little as possible. Scientists travel to the station on one of Great Britain's polar research ships. This is usually a 1,000-mile (1,600 km) journey from the Falkland Islands.

Seals on Bird Island

Penguins on South Georgia

⬅⬆ **SCIENTISTS** who work on Bird Island spend their time observing and recording the island's bird and seal populations. They gather data about numbers, feeding habits, and **breeding** behavior. Species of birds studied include albatrosses, penguins, and petrels.

By collecting this information, the scientists on Bird Island help to identify the threats to individual species from climate change and overfishing. They also monitor plastic pollution, which has become a deadly issue for the world's marine wildlife. If birds such as albatrosses eat too much plastic trash from the ocean, they may die.

The British Antarctic Survey's Halley Station is found on the coast of Antarctica at 75 degrees south. Scientists there have helped discover the effects of pollution on our planet. Today, researchers are helping to plan for the effects of climate change in the future.

Journey Across the ICE SHELVES

Halley Research Station, Antarctica

⬆ HALLEY RESEARCH STATION

is located on the Brunt Ice Shelf. The ice that makes up the shelf is 400 feet (122 m) thick. The station has eight buildings, which are home to 70 scientists in summer and 16 in winter. The buildings have adjustable legs with ski feet. Ice movement under the station is monitored by **GPS**. If necessary, the entire station can be taken apart and towed to a new location. This happened from 2016 to 2017, when a huge crack in the ice shelf threatened the station.

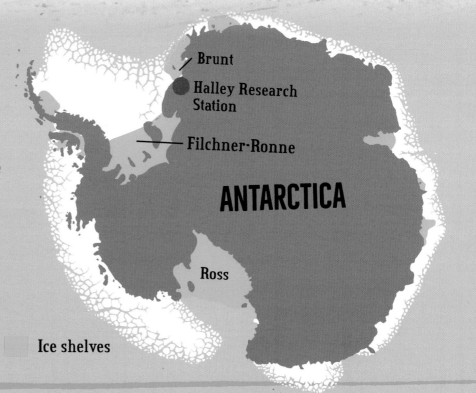

Brunt

Halley Research Station

Filchner-Ronne

ANTARCTICA

Ross

Ice shelves

The ozone layer

↓ THE AURORA AUSTRALIS is an amazing natural **phenomenon** that can be observed at Halley Research Station. The aurora takes the form of a glow in the night sky, or even shimmering curtains of light. These can be green, red, or other colors. Scientists study the aurora australis to try to understand how energy moves from the Sun toward Earth.

The aurora australis

↑ THE OZONE "HOLE" was discovered by scientists at Halley in the 1980s. Ozone is a gas that forms a thin layer in Earth's **atmosphere**. This protects us from **UV (ultraviolet) radiation** from the Sun, which can cause problems such as skin cancer and severe weather. Pollution from human-made chemicals caused the hole. After the hole was discovered, countries agreed to limit use of the chemicals. Scientists now estimate the ozone layer could recover by 2050.

Scientists camping on the ice, Berkner Island

↑ RESEARCH PROJECTS at Halley watch Antarctica's ice shelves. Global warming may be causing the shelves to weaken and break up. If this happens, sea levels around the world will rise, causing floods and damage. To do this fieldwork, researchers travel by air from Halley to camp on the Filchner-Ronne Ice Shelf. They drill through the ice with hot-water drills to take the temperature of the sea underneath, sample the water, and investigate the water currents under the ice. They also measure ice movement.

Pause for REFLECTION

- What does the story of the ozone hole highlight to you?
- Why do you think it is important to monitor Antarctica's ice shelves?

Cruise to the ANTARCTIC PENINSULA

Today, tourists from all over the world travel to Antarctica, marveling at the region's amazing scenery and wildlife. But growing tourist numbers could threaten Antarctica's fragile environment.

Most tourists begin their Antarctic adventure by flying to port cities such as Buenos Aires or Ushuaia in Argentina, or Punta Arenas in southern Chile. Australia and New Zealand are also departure points for Antarctic tourist ships.

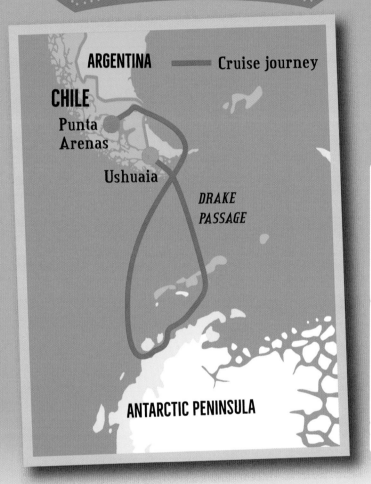

ARGENTINA — Cruise journey

CHILE

Punta Arenas

Ushuaia

DRAKE PASSAGE

ANTARCTIC PENINSULA

▼ **PASSENGER SHIPS** for Antarctic tourists are specially strengthened to protect against the ice. The ships leave Argentina or Chile, sail south across the Antarctic Circle, then head across the Drake Passage. In the surrounding seas, tourists can spot minke, humpback, and orca whales. Once at their destination, tourists can use small "Zodiac" boats to land on the ice shelf. There, they can hike, kayak, snorkel, and even camp. Tourists can also film and photograph penguins, seabirds, and seals.

A tourist ship and Antarctic penguins

Tourist ship near the Antarctic Peninsula

◀ **RESTRICTING SHIP SIZES** and numbers of landings also help protect the creatures living in Antarctica from human disturbance. There is evidence from the areas around research stations that Antarctic breeding birds will abandon their traditional nesting sites if too much human activity takes place nearby. Keeping tourist numbers down also helps lessen the chances that **invasive** plants from other countries could be accidentally introduced to Antarctica's fragile environment.

▶ **ANTARCTIC TOURISM** has grown massively in the last 20 years. In the 2002–2003 season, just 13,500 tourists visited the continent. By 2016–2017, this number had risen to 36,900. Most tourists come from the United States, China, Australia, and Germany. Antarctic tourism companies are controlled, in order to protect the continent. For example, the size of ships and the numbers of tourists who land every year are limited. Since 2009, large cruise ships carrying more than 500 passengers have been banned from Antarctic waters because of the fear of oil spills, which would pollute the seas.

A tourist photographs a penguin

PEOPLE ALONG THE WAY

Tourist cruises face the same danger from storms and ice as other ships in Antarctica. In 2007, a small cruise ship called the MV *Explorer* sailed too quickly into a dangerous ice field. The inexperienced captain did not realize how hard the Antarctic ice was. The ship hit the ice and started to sink. Fortunately for the 155 passengers and crew, the seas were calm, and other ships were able to come to the rescue. The ship sank, but everyone on board made it to safety.

Shipping SOUTH FROM SHANGHAI

Antarctica is shared by all countries. Some nations have had bases on the continent since the time of Amundsen and Scott. Great Britain, Norway, and the United States are among them. Since then, other countries have worked hard to have a presence in Antarctica. One such country is China.

↓ **CHINA'S SCIENTISTS** made their first Antarctic expedition in 1984. Today, China has four Antarctic research stations. The oldest station, named Great Wall, was built in 1985. This was followed by Zhongshan in 1989, Kunlun in 2009, and Taishan in 2014. China is currently planning a fifth station near the Ross Sea.

Like 53 other countries, including Canada and the United States, China has signed the Antarctic Treaty. This international agreement was created in 1959 in order to manage Antarctica for the future. The treaty states that research in Antarctica is for peaceful reasons only. Other agreements protect wildlife and the environment—for example, by banning the dumping of trash.

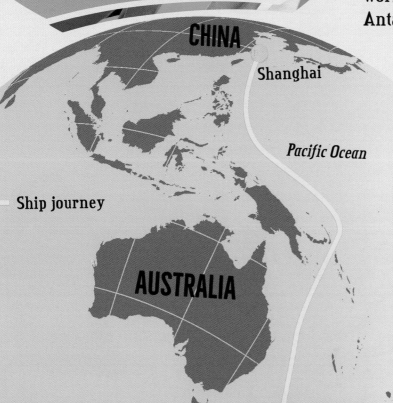

CHINA
Shanghai
Pacific Ocean
Ship journey
AUSTRALIA
Southern Ocean
NEW ZEALAND
Christchurch
Zhongshan
Great Wall
Taishan
Kunlun
ANTARCTICA
Ross Sea

Chinese research robot in Antarctica

TAISHAN STATION is China's newest research station. It sits at a height of more than 8,500 feet (2,590 m) above sea level, in an area that is continually blasted by freezing winds and blizzards. The research station building looks like a red Chinese lantern. It provides summer-only housing for 20 scientists. They study climate change, glaciers, **geology**, and Earth's atmosphere. Taishan uses wind and solar power to reduce the station's impact on the environment.

Taishan Station

CHINA'S RESEARCH SHIP, MV *Xue Long,* or "Snow Dragon," was originally built in 1993 as an Arctic cargo ship, able to break through ice. Later, it was bought by China and changed to make it into a polar research and resupply vessel. It now travels to and from China and Antarctica. A new research ship, the *Xue Long 2,* will soon enter service.

Chinese Antarctic expeditions sail from the Chinese port city of Shanghai, then cross the Pacific Ocean and head to Christchurch in New Zealand. There, they pick up additional supplies and personnel. Then they make the journey onward to Zhongshan Station, China's "gateway" base in Antarctica, which is on the Amery Ice Shelf in East Antarctica.

The MV *Xue Long* breaks through ice
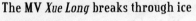

Pause for REFLECTION

- Antarctica is shared by all countries. Do you think any country or person should be able to "own" any land in Antarctica?

- Do you think it would be right for countries to use Antarctica's natural resources, for example, by fishing or by mining?

Researching CLIMATE CHANGE

Melting ice, Antarctic Peninsula

One of the biggest threats to Antarctica is climate change. But because of its unique unspoiled environment, Antarctica is also one of the best places on Earth for scientists to learn about the effects of climate change and predict how it will affect Earth in the future.

ANTARCTICA

↑ **ANTARCTIC ICE** contains up to 62 percent of the world's freshwater. As Earth's temperature warms, this ice is melting. A 2016 study by the University of Edinburgh found that if the West Antarctic ice sheet melted, then world sea levels might rise by up to 10 feet (3 m). This would put many low-lying areas of our planet underwater—a disaster affecting hundreds of millions of people.

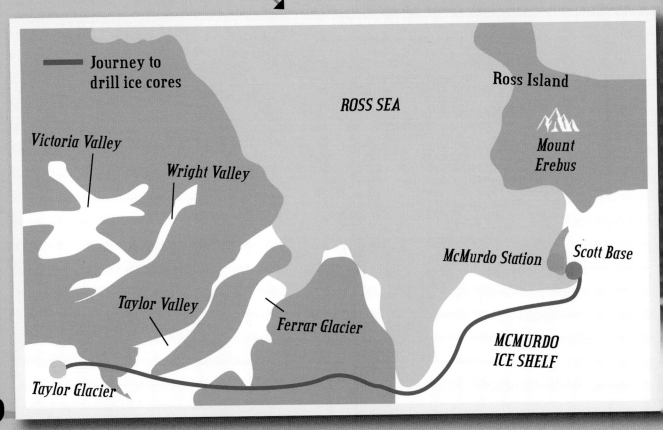

— Journey to drill ice cores

ROSS SEA

Ross Island

Victoria Valley

Wright Valley

Mount Erebus

McMurdo Station

Scott Base

Taylor Valley

Ferrar Glacier

MCMURDO ICE SHELF

Taylor Glacier

Penguins nesting, Antarctic Peninsula

↑ **THE ANTARCTIC PENINSULA** area is one of the fastest-warming areas of the continent. There, temperatures have risen by up to 5°F (2.8°C) over the last 50 years. Nearby ocean temperatures have risen by nearly 2°F (1.1°C). Glaciers are melting, and the region's ice shelves are quickly disappearing. This part of Antarctica is warming at up to five times faster than other parts of the world. The ice loss that results could have serious effects on Antarctic wildlife, with animal habitats shrinking or disappearing forever.

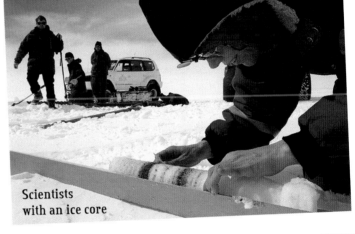

Scientists with an ice core

↑ **ICE CORING** is one important climate-change project. Scientists travel from New Zealand's Scott Base, near the Ross Sea, to the Taylor Glacier. There, they drill **ice cores** from the ice. Their goal is to find ancient air bubbles.

Air bubbles trapped in the ice can be 10,000 to 20,000 years old. Inside the air bubbles are gases that were present in the air at the time it was trapped. Scientists look for the gases that cause global warming. They measure the amount of these gases inside the air bubbles. Then, they use the data to create models of what Earth's climate was like in different time periods.

Scientists can test these models to see how Earth's climate might respond in different conditions. This helps them predict how Earth's climate might change in the future.

PEOPLE ALONG THE WAY

Damien is a research scientist at the Scott Base. He makes regular journeys to drill ice cores, traveling across the ice in a specially adapted tractor. The weather conditions can be harsh, with strong winds and freezing temperatures. But he knows that his work is very important to help protect Earth and its people from climate change.

GLOSSARY

aerial photography Taking photos from the air

Antarctic Circle Earth's southernmost circle of latitude, found at 66 degrees south

Antarctic Plateau The raised, icy area in the middle of Antarctica that contains the South Pole

astronomy The study of space and the stars

atmosphere The layer of air surrounding Earth

base camp The headquarters of an expedition where supplies are kept

breeding In animals, producing young

climate change Change in climate patterns around the world due to global warming, or the gradual increase in Earth's temperature

commercial Concerned with earning money

expedition A journey of discovery

extinct When the last animal or plant of a species has died and no more exist to reproduce

food chains Groups of living things linked in a series in which each is a source of food for the next

frostbite A painful condition caused by parts of the body being frozen

geographic South Pole The southern endpoint of Earth's axis, the imaginary line around which it spins, found at 90 degrees south

geology The study of Earth's physical features, especially the rocks that make up its surface

glaciers Slow-moving masses or rivers of ice

global warming The rising average temperature on Earth, caused by too many "greenhouse gases," such as carbon dioxide, in the atmosphere

GPS Short for Global Positioning System. A navigation system that uses signals from satellites to map an area.

hull The main body of a ship

ice cores Long cylinders of ice, usually 4–6 inches (10-15 cm) in diameter, which are removed from a thick, permanent sheet of ice

ice shelves Thick masses of ice at the edge of Antarctica. Ice sheets are usually connected to the ice on land, but float on the sea.

Inuit The native inhabitants of the Arctic region

invasive Describes a nonnative species that has been introduced deliberately or accidentally to a certain place and which threatens life already there

latitude A measure of distance from the equator, an imaginary line which is an equal distance from the North and South Poles

marine biologist A scientist who studies life in the oceans and seas

natural resources Useful or valuable materials and substances in nature, such as trees or gold

naval officer In the Navy, a sailor who is in charge of other sailors on a ship or boat

parka A warm coat with a hood and special lining to protect the wearer from extreme cold

phenomenon An event that occurs in nature

plankton Tiny plants and animals that float in the ocean and which form the basis of many food chains

reinforced Given extra strength

samples Small parts taken for examination

satellite A machine placed in space that circles, or orbits, Earth for the purpose of gathering information or for communication

scurvy A deadly disease caused by a lack of vitamin C in the diet

sleds Vehicles designed to transport loads on snow

sonar An underwater imaging system that uses sound waves to reveal features on the seabed

supply depots Piles of food, fuel, and other supplies left to be collected in the future

surveying Measuring and precisely recording Earth's geographical features

UV radiation A part of light that we cannot see

Further INFORMATION

BOOKS

Petersen, Christine. *Learning about Antarctica*. Lerner Publishing Group, 2015.

Rockett, Paul. *Mapping Australia and Oceania, and Antarctica*. Crabtree Publishing, 2017.

Seiple, Samantha. *Byrd & Igloo: A Polar Adventure*. Scholastic Press, 2013.

Walker, Sally M. *Frozen Secrets: Antarctica Revealed*. Carolrhoda Books, 2010.

WEBSITES

www.usap.gov
This is the web portal of the United States Antarctic Program.

www.ats.aq/e/ats.htm
Find out more about the Antarctic Treaty and how it aims to protect Antarctica.

https://climate.nasa.gov
Check out information from NASA about climate change and its effect on Earth and its people.

INDEX

ABOUT THE AUTHOR

John C. Miles studied classical music, history, and English, before working as an editor and writer of children's nonfiction books. Through his work, John has been able to pursue his love of writing about geography, history, and travel.